META MARKETING MASTERY

Mastering Facebook for Unstoppable Business Growth

Preface

In the ever-evolving landscape of digital marketing, few platforms have reshaped the way businesses connect with their audiences quite like Facebook. With over two billion active users, Facebook isn't just a social network; it's a powerful marketplace, a branding tool, and a global stage where businesses of all sizes compete for attention.

Yet, mastering Facebook marketing isn't merely about boosting posts or running ads. It requires understanding its dynamic ecosystem, leveraging its algorithms, and crafting strategies that resonate authentically with users. Whether you're a seasoned marketer seeking fresh insights or a beginner aiming to harness this platform's potential, this e-book is your comprehensive guide.

Meta Marketing Mastery delves into the nuances of building impactful campaigns, optimizing ad spend, and creating content that converts. With real-world examples and actionable tips, this book bridges the gap between theory and application.

As you embark on this journey, remember: success on Facebook is about more than metrics—it's about building relationships and delivering value. Let's unlock the secrets to thriving in the world of Facebook marketing together.

— Arjun Thakur

About the Author

Arjun Thakur is an experienced digital marketer, business strategist, and author passionate about empowering businesses to thrive in the digital age. With extensive expertise in running high-conversion Facebook and Instagram campaigns, Arjun has become a trusted guide for entrepreneurs and marketers seeking to master social media advertising.

In his debut book, **"Meta Marketing Mastery,"** Arjun combines years of professional experience and cutting-edge research to offer a comprehensive guide for leveraging Facebook's advertising ecosystem. This book provides actionable strategies to create cost-effective campaigns, optimize targeting with AI tools, and maximize ROI, all while maintaining clarity and accessibility.

Arjun's relatable tone and step-by-step approach ensure that readers, from beginners to seasoned marketers, can harness the full potential of Meta platforms. More than a guide to digital marketing, **"Meta Marketing Mastery"** is a transformative resource designed to help businesses achieve sustainable growth in the ever-evolving online marketplace.

— Arjun Thakur

Acknowledgements

I owe my deepest gratitude to my parents, whose unwavering love, guidance, and support have laid the foundation of my life and brought me into this beautiful world. Their belief in me has been my greatest source of strength and inspiration.

A heartfelt thanks to my beloved spouse, Hemlata, whose encouragement and patience have been my anchor during the creative journey of writing **"Meta Marketing Mastery."** To my sons, Mukul and Mehul, and my daughter, Riya, I am deeply grateful for their invaluable insights, shared enthusiasm, and assistance in shaping this book. Your love and support have been instrumental in making this project a reality.

Above all, I bow in reverence to my Master, whose wisdom and guidance have instilled meaning and purpose in my life. Your teachings have been the guiding light in my professional and personal journey, making this endeavour possible.

Lastly, my sincere thanks to the global humanitarian organization, **The Art of Living**, for imparting profound lessons on living a truly healthy and balanced life. Your philosophy has deeply influenced my approach to work, life, and the principles shared in this book.

This book, **"Meta Marketing Mastery,"** is a tribute to all of you—a reflection of the love, wisdom, and strength you have bestowed upon me. Thank you for being an integral part of this journey.

---Arjun Thakur

Contents

Preface 1
About the Author 2
Acknowledgements 3
1. Introduction: Why This Book Matters 7
   Purpose of the Book 7
   Who This Book is For 9
2. Why Facebook Campaigns Are a Must for Every Business ... 12
   The Global Advantage 12
   Impactful and Versatile 13
   Cost-Effective Advertising 17
3. The Blueprint for Campaign Success 19
   Setting Goals That Drive Results 19
   Mastering Your Target Audience 22
   Building a Winning Content Strategy 26
4. Harnessing the Power of AI in Facebook Advertising 30
   AI for Smart Campaigns 30
   Personalization at Scale 33
   Future AI Trends 36
5. A Step-by-Step Guide to Launching Campaigns 39
   Setting Up Your Ad Account 39
   Choosing the Right Ad Format 41
   Budgeting and Bidding Strategies 45
   A/B Testing for Perfection 47
6. Advanced Strategies for Game-Changing Campaigns 50
   Retargeting Done Right 50

- Lookalike Audiences: Your Growth Multiplier 53
- Seasonal and Event-Based Campaigns 54
- Geo-Targeting Techniques 56

7. Tracking Performance and Measuring Success 60
- Key Metrics Demystified 60
- Analytics for Continuous Improvement 62
- Scaling for Growth 64

8. Secrets to Achieving Cost Efficiency 67
- Optimizing ROI 67
- Scaling Without Breaking the Bank 68
- Avoiding Costly Mistakes 71

9. Troubleshooting Common Challenges 74
- Overcoming Ad Fatigue 74
- Policy Compliance Simplified 75
- Navigating Algorithm Changes 78

10. Real-World Success Stories 81
- Inspirational Case Studies 81

11. The Future of Meta Campaigns 85
- Emerging Trends 85

12. Final Thoughts: Your Roadmap to Success 89
- Summarize the core principles of creating and managing successful campaigns. 89
- Encourage your leads (prospective customers) to take immediate action and embrace experimentation. 91
- Closing motivational words to inspire long-term success. 93
- Call to Action: 94
- FREE Bonus 94

Additional Sections 94

Comprehensive Guide to Signing Up and Setting Up a Meta Business Manager Account 95

Introduction 95

Step 1: Prerequisites Before You Begin 95

Step 2: Signing Up for Meta Business Manager 95

Step 3: Setting Up Your Business Manager Account 96

Step 4: Integrating Instagram Accounts 98

Step 5: Verifying Your Business 99

Step 6: Organizing Assets for Efficient Management 99

Step 7: Setting Up Pixels and Events 99

Step 8: Securing Your Business Manager Account 100

1. Introduction: Why This Book Matters

Purpose of the Book

- **Explore why mastering *Meta Facebook Campaigns* is essential for business growth today.**

    Mastering Meta Facebook Campaigns is no longer a luxury but a necessity for modern business growth. With over **2.9 billion monthly active users**, Facebook (and its associated platforms like Instagram and Messenger) offers businesses an unparalleled opportunity to connect with a diverse and engaged audience. By leveraging Meta's advanced advertising tools, businesses can create highly targeted campaigns, ensuring their messages reach the right people at the right time.

    Meta campaigns go beyond basic advertising; they allow businesses to:

    Achieve Precision Targeting: By using demographics, behaviours, interests, and lookalike audiences, you can tailor campaigns to resonate with specific customer segments.

    Maximize ROI: Meta's AI-driven tools, such as ad optimization and budget allocation, help businesses stretch every dollar.

    Stay Competitive: As more businesses turn to digital advertising, mastering Meta campaigns ensures you remain relevant and visible in a crowded market.

    Build Brand Trust: Authentic storytelling through engaging ads strengthens relationships with customers and fosters long-term loyalty.

For businesses seeking growth, learning to navigate and master Meta's advertising platform is akin to mastering the modern-day language of marketing—a skill set that can dramatically transform visibility, engagement, and profitability.

- **How this book empowers readers to create impactful campaigns effortlessly.**

This book is designed to empower readers by simplifying the process of creating impactful Meta Facebook campaigns, transforming what might seem complex into an accessible and straightforward experience. It provides:

Clear Step-by-Step Guidance: Whether you're a beginner or an experienced advertiser, the book breaks down every stage of campaign creation—from setting goals to tracking performance—into actionable steps that anyone can follow.

Practical Tools and Techniques: With real-world examples, templates, and tips, readers can implement proven strategies without spending countless hours figuring out the details themselves.

Simplified Technical Concepts: The book demystifies technical aspects like AI-driven optimization, retargeting, and audience segmentation, presenting them in plain language that's easy to grasp and apply.

Focus on Efficiency: Learn to craft campaigns that maximize results while minimizing costs, making it easier to achieve high returns even with modest budgets.

By the end of the book, readers will feel confident in their ability to create campaigns that drive results, all while saving time, money, and effort. It's a roadmap to success, tailored for today's fast-paced digital marketing landscape.

Who This Book is For

- **Entrepreneurs, digital marketers, and small-to-medium business owners.**

    When we mention **entrepreneurs, digital marketers, and small-to-medium business owners (SMBs)**, we're addressing three key groups that fuel economic innovation and growth:

    Entrepreneurs: Visionaries who drive innovation, often starting from scratch. They face the challenge of making their brand visible in competitive markets with limited resources. For them, mastering Meta Facebook Campaigns provides a cost-effective, scalable solution to reach their target audience and establish a foothold in their industry.

    Digital Marketers: Professionals focused on connecting brands with their audience in meaningful ways. They constantly seek tools and strategies to enhance campaign performance, increase engagement, and maximize ROI. Meta's platform offers advanced features like audience targeting, retargeting, and AI-driven insights, making it a powerful asset for marketers.

    Small-to-Medium Business Owners: The backbone of local and global economies, SMBs often operate with limited budgets and resources. Meta campaigns allow them to compete with larger players by offering precise targeting, measurable results, and cost-efficient advertising options that amplify their reach without breaking the bank.

Each of these groups stands to benefit immensely from mastering Meta Facebook Campaigns, as it equips them with the tools to connect, grow, and thrive in today's digital-first economy.

- **Ideal for beginners and experienced professionals aiming to refine their skills.**

This book caters to a wide spectrum of readers, making it valuable for both **beginners** taking their first steps into the world of Meta Facebook Campaigns and **experienced professionals** seeking to refine their skills.

For Beginners: It provides a clear, step-by-step guide, breaking down complex concepts into simple, actionable insights. You'll learn everything from setting up your first campaign to understanding audience targeting and optimizing for performance. It demystifies the process, ensuring a confident start to leveraging Meta platforms effectively.

For Experienced Professionals: The book dives deeper into advanced strategies and techniques, offering fresh perspectives on AI integration, retargeting, and campaign scaling. It's packed with practical tips, real-world examples, and insights that can help even seasoned marketers enhance their results and stay ahead of the competition.

By catering to all levels, this book serves as a comprehensive resource for mastering Meta Facebook Campaigns, regardless of your starting point.

2. Why Facebook Campaigns Are a Must for Every Business

The Global Advantage

- **Facebook as a marketing giant with 2+ billion active users worldwide.**

  A Global Social Media Giant: Facebook boasts a massive user base of over 2 billion active users worldwide.
  Connecting the World: It serves as a digital hub for individuals to connect with friends, family, and like-minded people.
  A Powerful Marketing Tool: Businesses leverage Facebook's vast audience to build brand awareness, generate leads, and drive sales through targeted advertising and engaging content.
  Data Privacy Concerns: The platform's extensive data collection practices have raised concerns about user privacy and security.
  Algorithmic Influence: Facebook's algorithms shape our news feeds, potentially influencing our opinions and behaviours.
  Misinformation and Hate Speech: The platform has been criticized for its role in the spread of misinformation and hate speech.
  A Double-Edged Sword: While Facebook offers numerous benefits, it's essential to navigate its complexities and use it responsibly.

- **How its ecosystem (including Instagram and Messenger) amplifies reach.**

  Expanded Reach: Instagram and Messenger, as integral parts of Facebook's ecosystem, significantly expand its reach and influence.

Visual Storytelling: Instagram, with its emphasis on visual content, allows businesses and individuals to connect with audiences in a more engaging and visually appealing manner.

Direct Communication: Messenger enables direct and personalized communication with users, fostering stronger relationships and providing timely customer support.

Cross-Platform Integration: Seamless integration between Facebook, Instagram, and Messenger allows for consistent branding and messaging across different platforms.

Shared User Base: The shared user base of these platforms amplifies the potential reach of content and campaigns, maximizing exposure.

Data-Driven Insights: By leveraging data from multiple platforms, businesses can gain deeper insights into user behaviour and preferences, enabling more targeted and effective marketing strategies.

Impactful and Versatile

- **Tailored solutions for every business objective—brand awareness, lead generation, and sales etc.**

The campaign objectives for Facebook Ads help advertisers to align their ad strategies with their business goals. Here are the key campaign objectives:

1. **Brand Awareness**:
    - **Goal**: Increase the reach and visibility of your brand to as many people as possible.
    - **Usage**: Suitable for introducing a new brand or product to a wide audience.

2. **Reach:**

- **Goal**: Deliver your ads to as many people as possible.
- **Usage**: Used when the main goal is to maximize reach without focusing on engagement or conversions.

3. **Traffic**:
   - **Goal**: Drive people to a website or app.
   - **Usage**: Ideal for campaigns aimed at increasing visits to a specific page.

4. **Engagement**:
   - **Goal**: Encourage people to engage with your content by liking, commenting, or sharing your posts.
   - **Usage**: Best for posts that require a high level of interaction, such as posts involving contests or community engagement.

5. **App Installs**:
   - **Goal**: Increase the number of app installs or in-app engagements.
   - **Usage**: Suitable for apps that require a significant amount of traffic to grow their user base.

6. **Lead Generation**:
   - **Goal**: Collect contact information from people interested in your business.

- **Usage**: Ideal for collecting leads for sales follow-ups.

7. **Messages**:
    - **Goal**: Encourage people to send messages to your business.
    - **Usage**: Best for businesses that want to communicate directly with potential customers through Facebook Messenger.

8. **Conversions**:
    - **Goal**: Drive people to take valuable actions on your website, like purchases, sign-ups, or downloads.
    - **Usage**: Effective for businesses with a clear goal for users to complete specific actions on their websites.

9. **Catalog Sales**:
    - **Goal**: Promote items from your Facebook product catalog.
    - **Usage**: Useful for e-commerce businesses to display products directly to their target audience on Facebook.

Each objective is designed to help businesses meet specific goals, ensuring they get the most out of their advertising budget on Facebook.

Combining creativity with precision targeting for unmatched results in Facebook campaigns involves blending artistic vision with strategic precision. Creativity is the heartbeat of compelling content—captivating visuals, engaging stories, and authentic messaging that capture attention and spark interest. Meanwhile, precision targeting ensures this content reaches the right audience at the right moment.

Creativity: Engaging ads are not just about aesthetics but about creating an emotional connection with the audience. High-quality visuals, compelling narratives, and interactive formats like videos and carousels make ads memorable and shareable. By leveraging storytelling and visually appealing content, businesses can differentiate themselves from competitors and forge deeper connections with potential customers.

Precision Targeting: Facebook's advanced targeting tools allow marketers to define and refine their audience based on demographics, interests, behaviours, and even location. This means ads can be tailored not just to who you want to reach but to when and where they are most likely to engage. Combining this with creative ad formats means your message can be hyper-relevant, timely, and aligned with users' interests and activities.

Together, these elements enhance the effectiveness of Facebook campaigns, ensuring that creative ads are not only seen but also engage, convert, and build lasting relationships with your audience. This dual approach maximizes ROI and drives unparalleled results, making it an indispensable strategy for businesses looking to thrive in the digital landscape.

Cost-Effective Advertising

- **Case studies highlighting ROI achieved with even modest ad budgets.**

    ad budgets illustrate the power of Facebook campaigns to deliver significant results regardless of the initial investment. Businesses of all sizes have leveraged Facebook's advanced targeting options and ad formats to achieve impressive returns on their ad spend.

    For instance, a small local business might start with a modest budget of $5 to $10 per day on Facebook ads, targeting a highly specific audience segment. Case studies have shown that even with limited budgets, businesses can see a substantial return on investment (ROI) by driving more foot traffic, boosting sales, or increasing online engagement.

    A [report](#) **by Facebook** revealed that small businesses often experience a 3x return on ad spend with targeted campaigns. These case studies demonstrate that Facebook's precise audience targeting allows businesses to reach their most valuable customers without needing a large budget. The platform's ability to optimize ad performance based on user interactions helps maximize the impact of each dollar spent, making it an efficient and cost-effective marketing channel for businesses of all sizes 【[source](#)】 .

- How Facebook Ads outperform traditional media in cost efficiency.
- **How Facebook Ads outperform traditional media in cost efficiency**:

Facebook Ads offer superior cost efficiency compared to traditional media because they allow businesses to target specific audiences based on detailed demographics, interests, and behaviours. This precision targeting reduces wasted ad spend, ensuring that your ads reach the most relevant users. According to recent studies, Facebook ads can be up to **5 times more cost-efficient** than traditional forms of media like TV, radio, or print ads 【HT Media】 【Meta Facebook】 .

Moreover, Facebook's ad system supports a variety of bidding strategies, such as cost-per-click (CPC) and cost-per-impression (CPM), which allow businesses to manage their budgets more effectively. These options provide flexibility in how ads are priced and managed, leading to better control over advertising costs and maximizing the return on investment (ROI). Additionally, Facebook's algorithms continually optimize ad performance by adjusting placements, creative elements, and bids based on user engagement, further enhancing efficiency.

For businesses looking to maximize their marketing dollars, Facebook ads not only offer more targeted reach but also deliver a higher efficiency in cost management, making them a smart choice for budget-conscious marketers.

3. The Blueprint for Campaign Success
Setting Goals That Drive Results

- **Understanding campaign objectives: Awareness, Consideration, and Conversion.**

  Awareness:

  The primary goal at this stage is to introduce your brand, product, or service to a wide audience. It's about generating visibility and ensuring that people recognize and remember your brand. Strategies here focus on building a strong brand presence through high-reach channels like social media, display ads, or content marketing. Metrics such as impressions, reach, and brand recall are key indicators of success.

  Consideration:

  This stage targets audiences who are aware of your brand and encourages them to engage and explore more. The focus shifts to building trust, educating potential customers, and sparking interest. Tactics include offering detailed content like product demos, case studies, or testimonials. Metrics like website visits, video views, and engagement rates help measure effectiveness.

  Conversion:
  The final stage aims to turn interested prospects into paying customers or leads. The emphasis is on clear calls-to-action (CTAs) and reducing friction in the decision-making process. Campaigns might include retargeting ads, promotional offers, or streamlined checkout processes. Metrics like sales, lead submissions, and return on ad spend (ROAS) determine success.

Together, these objectives form a structured funnel, guiding customers from discovery to decision-making in a cohesive and effective marketing strategy.

- **Aligning business goals with the right Facebook ad solutions.**

To effectively leverage Facebook advertising, businesses must first clearly define their objectives. Once these goals are identified, the right ad solutions can be selected to maximize their impact. Here's a breakdown of common business goals and the corresponding Facebook ad solutions:

1. Brand Awareness:

Goal: Increase brand visibility and recognition.

Solution:

Brand Awareness campaigns

Reach and Frequency campaigns

2. Lead Generation:

Goal: Attract potential customers and capture their contact information.

Solution:

Lead Generation campaigns

Dynamic Ads (for retargeting)

3. Website Traffic:

Goal: Drive traffic to a specific website page or landing page.

Solution:

Traffic campaigns

Dynamic Ads (for retargeting)

4. App Promotion:

Goal: Increase app installs, re-engage existing users, or drive in-app actions.

Solution:

App Install campaigns

App Engagement campaigns

5. Sales:

Goal: Generate online sales or drive in-store purchases.

Solution:

Conversion campaigns

Dynamic Product Ads

Key Considerations for Effective Facebook Advertising:

Target Audience: Identify your ideal customer and create highly targeted ad sets.

Compelling Ad Creative: Use visually appealing images and persuasive copy.

Strong Call-to-Action: Encourage users to take the desired action.

Continuous Optimization: Monitor campaign performance and make adjustments as needed.

A/B Testing: Experiment with different ad variations to maximize results.

By aligning your business goals with the appropriate Facebook ad solutions, you can achieve significant growth and success.

Mastering Your Target Audience

- **The science of audience research and segmentation.**

    Audience research and segmentation are critical components of effective marketing strategies. By understanding your target audience, you can tailor your messaging and campaigns to resonate with them, leading to increased engagement and conversions.

    Audience Research

    Audience research involves gathering and analyzing data about your target audience. This data can include:

    Demographics: Age, gender, location, income, education, and occupation.

    Psychographics: Interests, hobbies, values, lifestyle, and attitudes.

    Behaviours: Purchase history, browsing habits, and social media activity.

    Audience Segmentation

Once you have a solid understanding of your target audience, you can segment them into smaller, more homogeneous groups. This allows you to tailor your marketing efforts to the specific needs and preferences of each segment.

Common segmentation strategies include:

Demographic Segmentation: Dividing the market based on demographic factors like age, gender, income, and location.

Psychographic Segmentation: Grouping customers based on their psychological traits, such as lifestyle, interests, and values.

Behavioural Segmentation: Segmenting customers based on their behaviour, such as purchase history, brand loyalty, and usage rate.

Benefits of Audience Research and Segmentation

Improved Targeting: More precise targeting of your marketing efforts.

Increased Relevance: More relevant and personalized messaging.

Higher Conversion Rates: Better conversion rates and customer satisfaction.

Enhanced Customer Experience: A more tailored and engaging customer experience.

Data-Driven Decision Making: Informed decision-making based on data and insights.

By investing in audience research and segmentation, businesses can gain a competitive edge and achieve sustainable growth.

- **Tips on leveraging demographics, behaviours, and interests effectively.**

To maximize the impact of your Facebook ads, it's crucial to deeply understand your target audience. By effectively leveraging demographics, behaviours, and interests, you can deliver highly relevant ads to the right people at the right time.

Here are some tips to help you get started:

1. Demographic Targeting:

Age: Target specific age groups to tailor your messaging accordingly.

Gender: Reach a specific gender to deliver gender-specific ads.

Location: Target users in specific geographic locations.

Language: Reach users who speak specific languages.

Education Level: Target users with specific education levels.

Household Income: Target users with specific income levels.

2. Behavioural Targeting:

Device Usage: Target users based on the devices they use (e.g., mobile, desktop).

Purchase Behaviour: Target users who have made purchases in the past.

App Usage: Target users who have installed specific apps.

Website Traffic: Target users who have visited your website.

Engagement: Target users who have engaged with your content (e.g., liked, commented, shared).

3. Interest Targeting:

Hobbies and Interests: Target users based on their hobbies and interests (e.g., sports, travel, technology).

Lifestyle: Target users based on their lifestyle (e.g., health-conscious, eco-friendly).

Digital Behaviours: Target users based on their online behaviour (e.g., frequent online shoppers, tech enthusiasts).

Additional Tips:

Combine Targeting Options: Use a combination of demographic, behavioural, and interest targeting to create highly specific audience segments.

Utilize Custom Audiences: Create custom audiences based on your existing customer data (e.g., email lists, website visitors) for more precise targeting.

Leverage Lookalike Audiences: Expand your reach by targeting users similar to your existing customers.

Test and Refine: Continuously test different targeting combinations to identify the most effective strategies.

Stay Updated: Keep up with Facebook's evolving targeting options and algorithm changes.

By effectively leveraging demographics, behaviours, and interests, you can create highly targeted Facebook ad campaigns that drive results.

Building a Winning Content Strategy

- **Creating scroll-stopping visuals and compelling ad copy.**

   To truly captivate your audience on Facebook, you need a powerful combination of visually striking ads and persuasive copy. Here's how to create both:

   Scroll-Stopping Visuals:

   High-Quality Images: Use sharp, clear images that are relevant to your product or service.

   Eye-Catching Videos: Short, engaging videos can grab attention and convey your message quickly.

   Strong Visual Hierarchy: Guide the viewer's eye to the most important information.

   Use of Color: Choose colors that evoke the desired emotions and align with your brand.

Minimalist Design: Keep your visuals clean and uncluttered.

Compelling Ad Copy:

Strong Headline: Grab attention immediately with a clear and concise headline.

Engaging Body Copy: Write concise, persuasive copy that highlights the benefits.

Clear Call-to-Action: Tell your audience what you want them to do (e.g., "Shop Now," "Learn More").

Use of Strong Verbs: Use action verbs to create a sense of urgency.

Personalization: Tailor your message to your target audience.

A/B Testing: Experiment with different ad copy variations to find the most effective.

Combining Visuals and Copy:

Consistency: Ensure your visuals and copy align with your brand's overall message.

Mobile-First: Optimize your ads for mobile devices.

Clear Value Proposition: Clearly communicate the value your product or service offers.

By focusing on creating visually appealing and persuasive ads, you can significantly improve your Facebook advertising campaigns.

- **The role of storytelling and authenticity in boosting engagement.**

    Storytelling and authenticity are powerful tools that can significantly boost engagement. Here's how:

    Storytelling:

    Emotional Connection: Stories evoke emotions, making content more memorable and relatable.

    Humanizing Brands: By sharing personal anecdotes and experiences, brands become more human and approachable.

    Improved Understanding: Stories simplify complex ideas, making them easier to comprehend.

    Increased Sharing: Engaging stories are more likely to be shared, expanding reach.

    Authenticity:

    Building Trust: Authenticity fosters trust, as audiences appreciate genuine and transparent communication.

    Creating Loyalty: Authentic brands build loyal customer bases who feel a deeper connection.

    Differentiation: In a crowded market, authenticity helps brands stand out.

    Positive Word-of-Mouth: Authentic experiences lead to positive word-of-mouth marketing.

    Combining Storytelling and Authenticity:

Share Personal Stories: Use first-person narratives to connect with your audience on a deeper level.

Be Transparent: Share both successes and failures to build credibility.

Use Visual Storytelling: Images, videos, and infographics can enhance the storytelling experience.

Encourage User-Generated Content: Empower your audience to share their own stories related to your brand.

By effectively combining storytelling and authenticity, businesses can create compelling content that resonates with their audience, drives engagement, and ultimately fosters long-lasting relationships.

4. Harnessing the Power of AI in Facebook Advertising

AI for Smart Campaigns

- **How Meta's machine learning optimizes ad delivery to maximize outcomes.**

    Meta's advertising platform relies heavily on advanced machine learning algorithms to optimize ad delivery and maximize outcomes. This sophisticated system analyzes vast amounts of data to make real-time decisions about which ads to show to which users, when, and at what price.

    Here's a breakdown of how it works:

    1. **Data Collection:** Meta collects data on user behaviour, preferences, and interactions with ads. This includes information like demographics, interests, device usage, and past purchase history.

    2. **Algorithm Development:** Machine learning models are trained on this data to identify patterns and predict user behaviour. These models can recognize which users are most likely to engage with a particular ad and take the desired action (e.g., click, purchase, install).

    3. **Real-Time Optimization:** As users interact with ads, the system continuously learns and adapts. It adjusts factors like bidding, targeting, and ad creative to improve performance. This includes:

        - **Automated Bidding:** The system automatically sets bids to maximize the desired outcome (e.g., clicks, conversions) within a specified budget.

- **Dynamic Creative Optimization:** The system tests different ad variations (e.g., images, headlines, copy) to identify the most effective combinations.
- **Audience Optimization:** The system continually refines the target audience to reach the most receptive users.

Benefits of Meta's Machine Learning:

Improved Targeting: Ads are delivered to the most relevant users, increasing engagement and conversion rates.

Enhanced Ad Performance: The system optimizes ad delivery in real-time to maximize ROI.

Increased Efficiency: Automation reduces the manual effort required to manage ad campaigns.

Personalized Experiences: Users are more likely to see ads that are relevant to their interests.

By leveraging machine learning, Meta's advertising platform helps businesses achieve their marketing goals more effectively and efficiently.

- **Examples of AI-enhanced tools like Dynamic Ads and Predictive Targeting.**

AI has revolutionized digital advertising, enabling precise targeting and personalized experiences. Two prominent examples of AI-enhanced tools are Dynamic Ads and Predictive Targeting.

1. Dynamic Ads:

Personalized Product Recommendations: Dynamic Ads leverage AI to automatically display relevant products to individual users based on their browsing history, purchase behaviour, and preferences.

Real-time Updates: These ads can be updated in real-time, ensuring that customers see the most current product information, pricing, and availability.

Improved Conversion Rates: By presenting highly relevant products, Dynamic Ads can significantly increase conversion rates and drive sales.

2. Predictive Targeting:

AI-Powered Audience Segmentation: Predictive Targeting utilizes AI algorithms to analyze vast amounts of data to identify potential customers who are likely to be interested in a product or service.

Accurate Predictions: By considering factors like demographics, interests, and online behaviour, AI can accurately predict future customer actions.

Efficient Resource Allocation: By focusing on high-potential audiences, businesses can optimize their advertising budgets and maximize ROI.

These AI-powered tools empower businesses to deliver highly targeted and personalized advertising campaigns, ultimately leading to better customer engagement and increased sales.

Personalization at Scale

- **Automating custom experiences for diverse customer segments.**

    Automating custom experiences involves leveraging technology to deliver tailored interactions that cater to the specific needs and preferences of different customer segments. This approach enhances customer satisfaction, loyalty, and ultimately, business growth.

    Key Strategies for Automation:

    Customer Segmentation: Divide your customer base into distinct groups based on shared characteristics like demographics, behaviours, or preferences.

    Personalized Communication: Utilize automation tools to send targeted emails, SMS messages, or push notifications with relevant content and offers.

    Dynamic Content: Employ personalization engines to dynamically adjust website content, product recommendations, and marketing messages based on individual customer data.

    AI-Powered Chatbots: Implement AI-driven chatbots to provide instant, personalized support and assistance, 24/7.

    Predictive Analytics: Analyze customer behaviour patterns to anticipate their needs and proactively offer relevant solutions.

Workflow Automation: Streamline customer journeys by automating repetitive tasks and decision-making processes.

Benefits of Automation:

Enhanced Customer Experience: Deliver more relevant and engaging interactions.

Increased Efficiency: Reduce operational costs and improve productivity.

Improved Customer Satisfaction: Meet customer needs more effectively.

Boosted Sales and Revenue: Drive conversions and upselling opportunities.

Data-Driven Insights: Gain valuable insights into customer behaviour for future optimization.

By embracing automation, businesses can create more personalized and efficient customer experiences, fostering stronger relationships and driving long-term success.

- **How AI adapts campaigns to user behaviours in real-time.**

AI revolutionizes digital marketing by empowering campaigns to evolve in real-time, based on user interactions. Here's a simplified breakdown of how this works:

1. Data Collection and Analysis:

AI-powered systems continuously gather vast amounts of data from various sources, including:

- Website visits
- App usage
- Social media interactions
- Email engagement
- Purchase history

This data is then analyzed to identify patterns, preferences, and emerging trends.

2. Real-Time Insights and Predictions:

AI algorithms process the collected data to generate actionable insights.

These insights can include:

- User segments with high purchase intent
- Optimal ad placements for maximum visibility
- Content that resonates best with specific audiences

AI can also predict future user behaviour, such as likely purchases or churn risk.

Dynamic Campaign Adjustments:

Based on real-time insights, AI can automatically adjust campaign elements:

- **Ad Creative:** Swapping out images, videos, or copy to improve engagement.
- **Targeting:** Refining audience segments to reach the most receptive users.

- **Bidding Strategy:** Optimizing bids to maximize conversions within budget constraints.
- **Ad Scheduling:** Adjusting the timing of ad delivery to capitalize on peak user activity.

4. Personalized User Experiences:

AI enables highly personalized experiences by tailoring content and offers to individual users.

This can include:

- **Personalized product recommendations:** Suggesting items based on browsing history and purchase behaviour.
- **Dynamic pricing:** Offering customized pricing based on user preferences and demographics.
- **Timely notifications:** Sending relevant alerts and reminders at the right moment.

By leveraging AI, marketers can deliver more effective, efficient, and engaging campaigns that drive better results.

Future AI Trends

- **What's next for AI in Facebook advertising— chatbots, AR/VR, and metaverse integration.**

  AI is poised to revolutionize Facebook advertising, and its integration with emerging technologies like chatbots, AR/VR, and the metaverse is set to redefine digital marketing. Here's a glimpse into the future:

1. AI-Powered Chatbots:

Personalized Customer Service: AI-driven chatbots can provide real-time, personalized customer support, answering queries and resolving issues efficiently.

Targeted Marketing: Chatbots can collect valuable user data, enabling highly targeted advertising campaigns.

2. AR/VR Advertising:

Immersive Brand Experiences: AR/VR can create immersive brand experiences, allowing users to interact with products in virtual environments.

Hyper-Personalized Ads: AI can analyze user behaviour in AR/VR to deliver highly personalized ads.

Metaverse Integration:

Virtual Brand Spaces: Brands can create virtual storefronts and experiences within the metaverse, offering unique shopping opportunities.

AI-Driven Product Recommendations: AI algorithms can analyze user preferences and behaviour in the metaverse to recommend products.

Key Benefits of AI Integration:

Enhanced User Experience: AI can provide personalized and seamless user experiences.

Increased Engagement: Immersive experiences drive higher engagement rates.

Improved Conversion Rates: AI-powered targeting and personalization can boost conversions.

Competitive Advantage: Early adoption of AI can give businesses a significant edge.

As AI continues to evolve, its integration with Facebook advertising will unlock new possibilities for brands to connect with their audience in innovative and impactful ways.

5. A Step-by-Step Guide to Launching Campaigns

Setting Up Your Ad Account

- **Navigating Business Manager, Ads Manager, and Meta Pixel with ease.**

    To effectively leverage Facebook's advertising ecosystem, understanding and navigating its primary tools is crucial. Here's a simplified breakdown of Business Manager, Ads Manager, and Meta Pixel:

    Business Manager:

    Central Hub: Serves as the central hub for managing your business's assets on Facebook.

    Key Functions:

    - **User Management:** Add and manage team members with specific permissions.
    - **Page and Ad Account Management:** Create and manage multiple pages and ad accounts.
    - **Asset Library:** Store and organize creative assets like images and videos.
    - **Security and Privacy:** Implement strong security measures to protect your business.

    Ads Manager:

    Campaign Creation and Management: The primary tool for creating, launching, and monitoring Facebook ad campaigns.

    Core Features:

- **Campaign Objective Selection:** Choose from various objectives like brand awareness, lead generation, or sales.
- **Audience Targeting:** Define your target audience based on demographics, interests, and behaviours.
- **Ad Creative Development:** Design compelling ad creatives, including images, videos, and text.
- **Budget Allocation:** Set daily or lifetime budgets and bidding strategies.
- **Performance Tracking:** Monitor key performance indicators (KPIs) like impressions, clicks, and conversions.

Meta Pixel:

Tracking and Optimization: A piece of code that tracks user behaviour on your website.

Benefits:

- **Audience Building:** Create custom audiences based on website visitors' actions.
- **Conversion Tracking:** Measure the effectiveness of your ad campaigns.
- **Retargeting:** Target users who have previously visited your website.
- **Event Optimization:** Optimize campaigns for specific actions like purchases or sign-ups.

Tips for Smooth Navigation:

Start Simple: Begin with a basic understanding of each tool and gradually explore advanced features.

Utilize Facebook's Help Center: Access detailed tutorials and troubleshooting guides.

Stay Updated: Keep up with the latest platform updates and best practices.

Experiment and Learn: Don't be afraid to try different strategies and analyze the results.

By mastering these tools, you can effectively manage your Facebook advertising campaigns and achieve your business goals.

Upload an image

This prompt requires an image that you need to add. Tap the image button to upload an image.

Got it

Choosing the Right Ad Format

- **Comprehensive guide to formats like Carousel, Video, Lead Ads, and Stories**.

Facebook offers a diverse range of ad formats, each designed to serve specific marketing objectives. Let's delve into some of the most popular ones:

1. Carousel Ads:

What are they? A series of images or videos that users can swipe through.

Best for: Showcasing multiple products or services, telling a story, or highlighting different features.

Why use them? They can increase engagement, brand awareness, and click-through rates.

2. Video Ads:

What are they? Short video clips that can be played with or without sound.

Best for: Telling a story, showcasing a product in action, or creating a strong emotional connection.

Why use them? They can capture attention, improve brand recall, and drive conversions.

Lead Ads:

What are they? A simplified mobile-friendly form that users can fill out directly within Facebook.

Best for: Capturing leads and generating interest in your products or services.

Why use them? They reduce friction in the lead generation process and increase conversion rates.

4. Story Ads:

What are they? Full-screen ads that appear in users' Stories feed.

Best for: Reaching a wide audience and driving immediate action.

Why use them? They offer a more immersive and engaging experience, and can be customized with interactive elements like polls and quizzes.

Choosing the Right Format:

When selecting a format, consider the following:

Your marketing goal: What do you want to achieve with your ad campaign?

Your target audience: What type of content will resonate with them?

Your budget: Some formats may be more expensive than others.

Your brand's aesthetic: Choose a format that aligns with your brand's image and messaging.

By understanding these formats and their strengths, you can create effective Facebook ad campaigns that deliver results.

- **Matching formats to business goals for maximum impact.**

To maximize the impact of your marketing efforts, it's crucial to align the right content format with your specific business goals. Here's a breakdown of common business goals and the content formats that can help you achieve them:

1. Brand Awareness:

Goal: Increase brand visibility and recognition.

Formats:

- **Social Media:** Engaging posts, visually appealing graphics, and short videos.
- **Blogging:** Thought leadership articles and industry news.
- **Video Marketing:** Brand stories, explainer videos, and behind-the-scenes footage.

2. Lead Generation:

- **Goal:** Attract potential customers and capture their contact information.
- **Formats:**
    - **Ebooks and Whitepapers:** In-depth content offering valuable insights.
    - **Webinars and Online Workshops:** Interactive sessions providing expert knowledge.
    - **Landing Pages:** Optimized pages designed to capture leads.

3. Customer Engagement:

- **Goal:** Build strong relationships with customers and foster loyalty.
- **Formats:**
    - **Email Marketing:** Personalized newsletters and promotional offers.
    - **Social Media:** Community building, contests, and polls.
    - **Customer Testimonials:** Showcase positive experiences.

4. Sales:

- **Goal:** Drive sales and increase revenue.
- **Formats:**

- **Product Demos and Trials:** Hands-on experiences.
- **Sales Pages:** Persuasive copy and strong calls to action.
- **Limited-Time Offers and Discounts:** Create urgency and drive immediate action.

Key Considerations for Content Format Selection:

Target Audience: Understand your audience's preferences and behaviours.

Platform: Choose platforms where your target audience is most active.

Content Calendar: Plan your content in advance to maintain consistency.

Analytics: Track performance metrics to measure success and make data-driven decisions.

By carefully selecting the right content formats and aligning them with your business goals, you can effectively engage your audience, drive conversions, and achieve sustainable growth.

Budgeting and Bidding Strategies

- **How to set realistic budgets and leverage auto-bidding effectively.**

  Setting Realistic Budgets

  1. **Define Clear Goals:**
     - **Brand Awareness:** Focus on reach and frequency metrics.

- **Lead Generation:** Prioritize clicks and conversions.
- **Sales:** Optimize for purchases and revenue.

2. **Consider Your Budget Constraints:**
    - **Daily Budget:** Allocate a specific amount to spend daily.
    - **Lifetime Budget:** Set a total budget for the entire campaign.

3. **Start Small, Scale Smart:**
    - **Pilot Campaigns:** Begin with smaller budgets to test performance.
    - **Iterate:** Adjust budgets based on results and insights.

Leveraging Auto-Bidding

1. **Understand Auto-Bidding Strategies:**
    - **Maximum Bid:** Set a maximum bid, and Facebook automatically bids within that limit.
    - **Target Cost Per Result (TCPA):** Specify a target cost per desired action (e.g., purchase, lead).
    - **Target Return on Ad Spend (TROAS):** Set a target return for every dollar spent on ads.

2. **Set Clear Bidding Goals:**
    - **Align with Business Objectives:** Ensure bidding strategies support overall goals.

- **Consider Campaign Type:** Choose the appropriate bidding strategy for each campaign.

3. **Monitor and Optimize:**
   - **Track Performance Metrics:** Regularly review key metrics like clicks, conversions, and cost per result.
   - **Make Adjustments:** Modify bids, budgets, and targeting as needed.

Tips for Effective Auto-Bidding:

Provide Sufficient Data: Ensure your campaigns have enough data for the algorithm to learn and optimize.

Set Realistic Expectations: Auto-bidding can take time to optimize, so be patient.

Combine Auto-Bidding with Manual Bidding: Use a hybrid approach for greater control.

Stay Informed: Keep up with the latest Facebook advertising updates and best practices.

By carefully setting realistic budgets and effectively leveraging auto-bidding, you can optimize your Facebook advertising campaigns for maximum ROI.

A/B Testing for Perfection

- **Simple techniques for testing creatives, audiences, and placements to find what works best**.

To optimize your Facebook ad campaigns, A/B testing is a powerful tool. By testing different variables, you can identify the most effective strategies to achieve your goals. Here are some simple techniques to get started:

1. Creative Testing:

Headline and Body Copy: Experiment with different headlines and body copy to see which ones resonate best with your audience.

Images and Videos: Test various visual elements, including images, videos, and GIFs.

Call-to-Action (CTA): Try different CTAs to see which ones drive the most conversions.

2. Audience Testing:

Demographics: Test different age groups, genders, and locations to find your ideal audience.

Interests and Behaviours: Experiment with targeting people based on their interests, behaviours, and purchase history.

Lookalike Audiences: Create lookalike audiences based on your best-performing customers to reach similar individuals.

3. Placement Testing:

Platform Placement: Test different platforms, such as Facebook News Feed, Instagram, and Messenger, to see where your ads perform best.

Device Placement: Test different devices, such as mobile and desktop, to optimize your ad delivery.

Tips for Effective A/B Testing:

Isolate Variables: Test only one variable at a time to accurately measure its impact.

Set Clear Goals: Define specific goals for your tests, such as increasing clicks, conversions, or sales.

Use Sufficient Sample Size: Ensure your tests have a large enough sample size to obtain statistically significant results.

Monitor Performance Closely: Track key metrics, such as click-through rates, conversion rates, and cost per acquisition.

Iterate and Optimize: Continuously analyze your test results and make adjustments to improve your campaigns.

By implementing these simple techniques, you can gain valuable insights into what works best for your business and achieve better results with your Facebook advertising efforts.

6. Advanced Strategies for Game-Changing Campaigns

Retargeting Done Right

- **Using Meta Pixel data to re-engage warm leads.**

  Meta Pixel, a powerful tool provided by Meta (formerly Facebook), allows businesses to track user behaviour on their websites and apps. This valuable data can be leveraged to re-engage warm leads, those who have already shown interest in your brand.

  Here's how Meta Pixel data can be used to re-engage warm leads:

1. **Custom Audience Creation:**

   Website Visitors: Create custom audiences based on website visitors who have viewed specific pages, added items to their cart, or initiated checkout processes.

   Event Completers: Identify users who have completed specific actions, such as signing up for a newsletter, downloading an ebook, or attending a webinar.

2. **Lookalike Audiences:**

   Expand your reach by creating lookalike audiences based on your existing customer or lead data. These audiences consist of users who share similar characteristics with your target audience.

3. **Retargeting Campaigns:**

Personalized Ads: Deliver highly targeted ads to warm leads based on their browsing history and past interactions.

Dynamic Ads: Showcase relevant products or services to users who have previously viewed them on your website.

Timely Reminders: Send timely reminders to users who have abandoned their carts or unfinished checkout processes.

4. **Conversion Tracking:**

   Monitor the effectiveness of your re-engagement campaigns by tracking conversions and calculating return on ad spend (ROAS).

   Optimize your campaigns by analyzing performance metrics and making data-driven adjustments.

   By effectively utilizing Meta Pixel data, businesses can nurture warm leads, increase conversions, and drive long-term customer loyalty.

- **Strategies for retargeting high-intent audiences.**

   Retargeting high-intent audiences is a powerful strategy to convert website visitors into customers. Here are some effective strategies to maximize your retargeting efforts:

   1. Identify High-Intent Behaviours:

   Product Page Visits: Users who spend significant time on product pages are likely to be interested in purchasing.

Cart Abandonment: Visitors who add items to their cart but don't complete the purchase are prime targets for retargeting.

Checkout Page Visits: Users who reach the checkout page but don't complete the transaction are highly qualified leads.

2. Create Personalized Ad Creative:

Dynamic Ads: Use dynamic ads to display specific products or offers that the user has previously viewed.

Personalized Messaging: Tailor your ad copy to the user's specific interests and behaviour.

Sense of Urgency: Use limited-time offers or countdown timers to create a sense of urgency.

3. Implement a Multi-Channel Retargeting Strategy:

Facebook and Instagram: Reach users on these platforms with visually appealing ads.

Google Ads: Target users with search ads and display ads on relevant websites.

Email Marketing: Send personalized email campaigns to re-engage users.

4. Utilize Lookalike Audiences:

Expand Your Reach: Create lookalike audiences based on your high-intent audience to identify similar users.

Increase Conversions: Target these lookalike audiences with highly relevant ads.

5. Track and Optimize Your Campaigns:

Monitor Key Metrics: Track metrics like click-through rate, conversion rate, and return on ad spend (ROAS).

A/B Test: Experiment with different ad creatives, targeting options, and bidding strategies to optimize performance.

Adjust Your Strategy: Continuously refine your retargeting campaigns based on data-driven insights.

By combining these strategies, you can effectively retarget high-intent audiences, increase conversions, and drive revenue for your business.

Lookalike Audiences: Your Growth Multiplier

- **Expanding your reach by targeting users similar to your best customers.**

    One of the most powerful strategies to expand your customer base is to target users who share similar characteristics with your existing, high-value customers. This technique, often referred to as "lookalike audiences," leverages advanced algorithms to identify potential customers who are likely to convert.

    How it works:

1. **Identify Your Best Customers:** Determine which segment of your customer base is most valuable.

This might be based on factors like purchase frequency, average order value, or customer lifetime value.

2. **Create a Custom Audience:** Upload a list of these high-value customers' email addresses or phone numbers to your advertising platform (like Facebook Ads or Google Ads).

3. **Build a Lookalike Audience:** The platform's algorithm analyzes the characteristics of your custom audience and identifies other users who share similar demographics, interests, and behaviours.

Benefits of Targeting Lookalike Audiences:

Increased Reach: Expand your audience beyond your current customer base.

Improved Targeting: Reach users who are highly likely to convert.

Higher ROI: Efficiently allocate your advertising budget to reach the most promising audience.

Enhanced Brand Awareness: Introduce your brand to new, qualified potential customers.

By effectively utilizing lookalike audiences, you can significantly boost your marketing efforts and drive sustainable business growth.

Seasonal and Event-Based Campaigns
- **Tapping into holidays, local events, and trends to supercharge engagement.**

Leveraging timely events and trends can significantly boost your social media engagement. Here are some strategies to capitalize on these opportunities:

1. Holiday Marketing:

Seasonal Content: Create relevant content that aligns with the holiday spirit, such as festive greetings, special offers, or holiday-themed contests.

Limited-Time Offers: Introduce exclusive deals or discounts to encourage immediate action.

User-Generated Content: Encourage your audience to share their holiday experiences using a branded hashtag.

2. Local Event Marketing:

Partner with Local Businesses: Collaborate with local businesses to cross-promote each other's offerings.

Sponsor Local Events: Support community events to increase brand visibility and goodwill.

Create Location-Specific Content: Tailor your content to the interests and preferences of your local audience.

Trending Topic Marketing:

Real-Time Marketing: Respond quickly to trending topics and news events with relevant and timely content.

Create Shareable Content: Develop engaging content that encourages sharing and viral spread.

Use Relevant Hashtags: Incorporate popular hashtags to increase discoverability.

Key Tips for Effective Event-Based Marketing:

Plan Ahead: Start planning your campaigns well in advance to ensure timely execution.

Stay Updated: Monitor social media trends and news to identify potential opportunities.

Use Analytics: Track the performance of your campaigns to measure their impact.

Personalize Your Approach: Tailor your messaging to resonate with your target audience.

Be Authentic: Avoid forced or inauthentic content that may alienate your audience.

By strategically incorporating holidays, local events, and trends into your social media strategy, you can elevate your brand's visibility, drive engagement, and ultimately achieve your marketing goals.

Geo-Targeting Techniques

- How to drive **local business success with precision targeting**.

    Precision targeting is a powerful tool that enables local businesses to reach their ideal customers with laser-like accuracy. By understanding and leveraging the capabilities of platforms like Facebook and Google Ads, businesses can significantly enhance their marketing efforts and drive local success.

Key Strategies for Precision Targeting:

1. **Geo-Targeting:**

    Benefit: Reach customers within a specific geographic radius.

    Implementation:
    - Set a target location (city, zip code, or radius around a specific address).
    - Utilize location-based keywords in ad copy and landing pages.

2. **Demographic Targeting:**

    Benefit: Reach customers based on age, gender, income, education, and other demographic factors.

    Implementation:
    - Leverage detailed demographic data provided by platforms.
    - Tailor ad messaging to specific demographics.

3. **Interest-Based Targeting:**

    Benefit: Reach customers based on their interests and hobbies.

    Implementation:
    - Use platforms' interest categories to identify relevant audiences.
    - Create ad content that aligns with their interests.

4. **Behaviour-Based Targeting:**

Benefit: Reach customers based on their online behaviour (e.g., website visits, app usage).

Implementation:

- Utilize retargeting ads to re-engage past visitors.
- Implement remarketing campaigns to remind customers of abandoned carts or incomplete purchases.

5. **Lookalike Audiences:**

Benefit: Expand your reach by finding new customers similar to your existing ones.

Implementation:

- Upload a list of your best customers to create a lookalike audience.
- Target these lookalike audiences with highly relevant ads.

Tips for Effective Precision Targeting:

Know Your Audience: Develop detailed customer personas to understand their needs and preferences.

Utilize Local SEO: Optimize your website and Google My Business listing for local search.

Leverage Social Media: Engage with your local community on platforms like Facebook, Instagram, and Twitter.

Monitor and Optimize: Continuously track campaign performance and make necessary adjustments.

Measure ROI: Calculate the return on investment (ROI) of your targeting efforts to assess their effectiveness.

By implementing these precision targeting strategies, local businesses can effectively reach their target audience, generate more leads, and drive sales.

7. Tracking Performance and Measuring Success

Key Metrics Demystified

- **CTR, CPC, ROAS, and the metrics that truly matter.**

    Understanding these key metrics is crucial for optimizing your digital advertising campaigns. Let's break them down:

    Core Metrics:

    CTR (Click-Through Rate): This measures the percentage of people who click on your ad after seeing it. A higher CTR indicates a more compelling ad.

    CPC (Cost Per Click): This is the average amount you pay for each click on your ad. A lower CPC means a more efficient campaign.

    ROAS (Return on Ad Spend): This metric calculates the revenue generated for every dollar spent on advertising. A higher ROAS indicates a profitable campaign.

    Beyond the Basics: The Metrics That Matter Most

    While CTR, CPC, and ROAS are essential, they don't tell the whole story. Here are some metrics that offer deeper insights:

    Conversion Rate: Measures the percentage of people who take a desired action (e.g., purchase, sign-up) after clicking on your ad.

Cost Per Acquisition (CPA): Calculates the cost of acquiring a customer or lead.

Customer Lifetime Value (CLTV): Estimates the total revenue a customer generates over their lifetime.

Engagement Rate: Measures how often people interact with your ad (likes, shares, comments).

Time on Site: Indicates how long visitors spend on your website after clicking your ad.

Why These Metrics Matter:

Conversion Rate: Directly impacts your bottom line.

CPA: Helps you set realistic budgets and measure campaign efficiency.

CLTV: Enables you to make informed decisions about customer acquisition costs.

Engagement Rate: Shows how relevant and interesting your ads are.

Time on Site: Suggests the quality of your landing pages and website content.

The Bottom Line:

While CTR, CPC, and ROAS are important starting points, focusing solely on these metrics can be misleading. By considering a broader range of metrics, you can gain a more accurate understanding of your campaign's performance and make data-driven decisions to optimize your strategy.

Analytics for Continuous Improvement

- **How to interpret data to fine-tune campaigns effectively.**

Data is the lifeblood of any successful marketing campaign. By understanding and interpreting data, you can make informed decisions to optimize your strategies. Here's a breakdown of how to effectively utilize data to fine-tune your campaigns:

1. Define Your KPIs:

Identify Key Metrics: Determine the metrics that matter most to your campaign goals. This could include clicks, impressions, conversions, or return on ad spend (ROAS).

Set Clear Objectives: Establish specific, measurable, achievable, relevant, and time-bound (SMART) goals.

2. Collect and Analyze Data:

Utilize Analytics Tools: Employ tools like Google Analytics, Facebook Ads Manager, or other platform-specific analytics to gather data.

Track Key Metrics: Monitor metrics regularly to identify trends and patterns.

Segment Your Audience: Break down your audience into smaller groups based on demographics, interests, or behaviours.

A/B Testing: Experiment with different ad variations to determine the most effective approach.

3. Interpret Data Insights:

Identify High-Performing Elements: Determine which ad creatives, targeting options, or landing pages are driving the best results.

Uncover Low-Performing Areas: Identify areas where your campaign is underperforming and allocate resources accordingly.

Analyze Customer Behaviour: Understand how your audience interacts with your ads and website to refine your messaging and offers.

4. Make Data-Driven Decisions:

Optimize Ad Spend: Allocate your budget to the most effective channels and ad placements.

Refine Targeting: Adjust your targeting criteria to reach the right audience.

Improve Ad Creatives: Create more compelling ad copy and visuals.

Enhance Landing Pages: Optimize your landing pages for conversions.

5. Continuously Monitor and Adjust:

Regularly Review Performance: Keep a close eye on your campaign metrics.

Iterate and Improve: Make ongoing adjustments based on data insights.

Stay Adaptable: Be prepared to pivot your strategy as needed to achieve your goals.

By following these steps and leveraging data-driven insights, you can fine-tune your campaigns for maximum impact and achieve better results.

Scaling for Growth

- **Identifying successful campaigns and replicating them at scale**.

To effectively scale successful campaigns, businesses must first identify which campaigns are truly driving results. Here's a step-by-step approach to identifying and scaling these campaigns:

1. Define Key Performance Indicators (KPIs):

Clearly define what constitutes a "successful" campaign.

Establish relevant KPIs like conversion rates, revenue generated, customer acquisition cost (CAC), or return on investment (ROI).

2. Analyze Campaign Performance:

Utilize analytics tools to track key metrics and identify trends.

Compare the performance of different campaigns to identify top performers.

Drill down into specific elements like ad copy, visuals, targeting, and landing pages to understand what works best.

3. Identify the Winning Formula:

Pinpoint the key factors that contributed to the success of the campaign.

Analyze the target audience, messaging, and creative elements that resonated with them.

Consider the timing and platform where the campaign was most effective.

4. Replicate the Winning Formula:

Create a standardized template for future campaigns, incorporating the successful elements.

Adapt the campaign to different target audiences or platforms while maintaining the core message and creative style.

Test and refine the replicated campaign to ensure it continues to deliver results.

5. Scale the Campaign:

Increase the budget to reach a wider audience.

Expand the target audience to include similar demographics or interests.

Utilize automation tools to streamline the campaign management process.

Monitor performance closely and make adjustments as needed.

6. Learn and Iterate:

Continuously analyze campaign performance to identify opportunities for improvement.

Experiment with new ideas and approaches to keep campaigns fresh and engaging.

Use data-driven insights to inform future campaign strategies.

By following these steps, businesses can effectively identify, replicate, and scale successful campaigns to drive growth and maximize ROI.

8. Secrets to Achieving Cost Efficiency
Optimizing ROI

- **Proven techniques to stretch every marketing dollar further.**

    In today's competitive landscape, maximizing your marketing budget is crucial. Here are some proven techniques to help you stretch every dollar further:

    1. Data-Driven Decision Making:

    Track and Analyze: Utilize analytics tools to monitor campaign performance.

    Identify High-Performing Channels: Allocate more budget to channels that yield the best results.

    A/B Testing: Experiment with different approaches to optimize your campaigns.

    2. Leverage Digital Marketing:

    Content Marketing: Create high-quality content that attracts and engages your target audience.

    SEO: Optimize your website to improve organic search rankings.

    Social Media Marketing: Build a strong online presence and engage with your audience.

    Email Marketing: Nurture leads and drive sales through targeted email campaigns.

    3. Build Strong Relationships with Influencers:

    Partner with Influencers: Collaborate with influencers in your niche to reach a wider audience.

Authentic Partnerships: Choose influencers who genuinely align with your brand values.

4. Utilize Affordable Marketing Tactics:

Public Relations: Leverage press releases, media outreach, and media relations.

Referral Marketing: Encourage satisfied customers to refer friends and family.

User-Generated Content: Encourage customers to share their experiences with your brand.

5. Optimize Your Marketing Spend:

Consolidate Vendors: Reduce costs by working with fewer vendors.

Negotiate Better Rates: Leverage your bargaining power to secure discounts.

Automate Tasks: Use marketing automation tools to streamline processes and save time.

By implementing these techniques, you can maximize your marketing ROI and achieve greater success with a limited budget.

Scaling Without Breaking the Bank

- **Strategic approaches to budget increases for steady campaign growth.**

    Securing increased budget for your marketing campaigns is a crucial step in driving business growth. Here are some strategic approaches to effectively advocate for and implement budget increases:

1. Demonstrate Clear ROI:

Quantify Results: Clearly articulate the tangible results achieved with the current budget, such as increased sales, leads, or website traffic.

Highlight Cost-Effectiveness: Showcase how your campaigns deliver a high return on investment (ROI) compared to other marketing channels.

Use Data-Driven Insights: Utilize data analytics to identify trends, optimize campaigns, and predict future performance.

2. Align with Business Goals:

Connect the Dots: Clearly demonstrate how your campaign goals directly contribute to the overall business objectives.

Highlight Strategic Importance: Emphasize the role of marketing in driving brand awareness, customer acquisition, and revenue generation.

Showcase Long-Term Value: Explain how increased budget will lead to sustainable growth and brand loyalty.

3. Propose Scalable Strategies:

Identify Growth Opportunities: Highlight untapped potential markets or product lines that can benefit from increased marketing investment.

Outline Scalable Tactics: Present specific strategies, such as expanding target audiences, increasing ad frequency, or launching new campaign channels.

Provide a Detailed Budget Breakdown: Clearly outline how the additional funds will be allocated to specific initiatives and their expected impact.

4. Build Strong Relationships:

Foster Open Communication: Maintain regular communication with key stakeholders, including executives and finance teams.

Seek Feedback and Input: Actively solicit feedback and incorporate suggestions to refine your campaign strategy.

Demonstrate Reliability and Trust: Consistently deliver on your promises and build a reputation as a reliable and effective marketer.

5. Leverage Industry Trends and Best Practices:

Stay Updated: Keep abreast of the latest marketing trends, technologies, and industry benchmarks.

Highlight Innovative Approaches: Showcase how your team is adopting innovative strategies to stay ahead of the competition.

Leverage Case Studies: Share successful case studies from other companies that have achieved significant growth through increased marketing investment.

By following these strategic approaches, you can effectively advocate for budget increases and drive sustained growth for your marketing campaigns.

Avoiding Costly Mistakes

- **Common pitfalls in budgeting and how to sidestep them.**

    Budgeting is a crucial financial tool, but even the most meticulous planners can fall into common traps. Here are some pitfalls to watch out for and strategies to avoid them:

    1. Underestimating Expenses:

    Pitfall: Failing to account for unexpected costs or underestimating regular expenses.

    Solution:

    - **Categorize Expenses:** Break down expenses into smaller categories to identify potential oversights.
    - **Review Past Spending:** Analyze previous spending patterns to identify recurring costs.
    - **Build a Contingency Fund:** Set aside a portion of your budget for unexpected expenses.

    2. Overestimating Income:

    Pitfall: Assuming a steady income stream without considering potential fluctuations or job losses.

    Solution:

    - **Be Realistic:** Base your budget on expected income, not hoped-for income.

- **Plan for the Worst:** Consider potential income reductions and adjust your budget accordingly.

3. Lack of Flexibility:

Pitfall: Sticking rigidly to a budget without room for adjustments.

Solution:

- **Regular Reviews:** Periodically review and adjust your budget as needed.
- **Prioritize:** Identify essential expenses and be flexible with non-essential ones.

4. Ignoring Debt Repayment:

Pitfall: Neglecting debt payments can lead to increased interest and financial stress.

- **Solution:**
  - **Prioritize Debt:** Allocate a portion of your budget to debt repayment.
  - **Create a Debt Repayment Plan:** Develop a strategy to pay off debts systematically.

5. Emotional Spending:

Pitfall: Making impulsive purchases based on emotions rather than needs.

- **Solution:**

- **Wait 24 Hours:** Pause before making a significant purchase to avoid impulsive decisions.
- **Track Emotional Spending:** Identify triggers for emotional spending and develop coping mechanisms.

By recognizing these common pitfalls and implementing effective strategies, you can create a budget that empowers your financial goals and provides peace of mind.

9. Troubleshooting Common Challenges

Overcoming Ad Fatigue

- **Techniques to keep campaigns fresh and engaging.**

To maintain audience interest and drive campaign success, it's essential to keep your content fresh and engaging. Here are some effective techniques:

1. Dynamic Content:

Personalized Experiences: Tailor content to individual user preferences and behaviours.

Real-Time Updates: Incorporate current events, trends, or time-sensitive offers.

2. Interactive Elements:

Polls and Quizzes: Encourage audience participation and gather valuable insights.

Contests and Giveaways: Create excitement and drive engagement.

Gamification: Transform routine actions into fun challenges.

3. Visual Storytelling:

High-Quality Imagery: Use visually appealing images and videos.

Infographics: Present complex information in a digestible format.

Short-Form Video: Utilize platforms like TikTok and Instagram Reels for quick, impactful storytelling.

4. Consistent Branding:

Brand Voice and Tone: Maintain a consistent brand identity across all channels.

Visual Consistency: Use a cohesive color palette and design elements.

5. Timely and Relevant Content:

Newsjacking: Leverage current events to create timely and relevant content.

Seasonal Campaigns: Adapt your content to holidays and seasonal trends.

6. A/B Testing:

Experimentation: Continuously test different approaches to optimize performance.

Data-Driven Decisions: Use insights to refine your strategy.

7. Collaborations and Partnerships:

Influencer Marketing: Partner with influential individuals to reach a wider audience.

Brand Collaborations: Collaborate with complementary brands to create unique campaigns.

By implementing these techniques, you can create campaigns that captivate your audience, drive conversions, and build long-lasting brand loyalty.

Policy Compliance Simplified

- **Practical advice to ensure your ads stay within Meta's guidelines.**

To avoid ad disapprovals and account restrictions, it's crucial to adhere to Meta's advertising policies. Here are some practical tips:

1. Understand the Guidelines:

Familiarize Yourself: Thoroughly review Meta's Advertising Policies to understand the dos and don'ts.

Stay Updated: Regularly check for policy updates to ensure compliance.

2. Quality Ad Creative:

High-Quality Images and Videos: Use clear, visually appealing, and high-resolution images and videos.

Accurate and Honest Content: Ensure your ad copy and visuals are truthful and accurate.

Avoid Shocking or Sensational Content: Refrain from using explicit, offensive, or misleading content.

3. Target Audience:

Precise Targeting: Use detailed targeting options to reach your ideal audience.

Avoid Discriminatory Targeting: Ensure your targeting criteria are not discriminatory or exclusive.

4. Landing Page Experience:

Relevant Landing Pages: Direct users to pages that are directly related to your ad content.

Clear and Easy Navigation: Make your landing pages user-friendly and easy to navigate.

Fast Loading Times: Optimize your landing pages for speed.

5. Ad Copy and Language:

Clear and Concise: Use clear and concise language in your ad copy.

Avoid Misleading Claims: Be honest and transparent in your messaging.

Adhere to Language Policies: Follow Meta's language policies and avoid prohibited languages.

6. Legal and Regulatory Compliance:

Comply with Laws: Ensure your ads comply with all applicable laws and regulations, including those related to privacy, consumer protection, and fair advertising.

Obtain Necessary Permissions: Obtain any necessary permissions or licenses for using copyrighted material or trademarks.

7. Monitor and Optimize:

Regularly Monitor: Keep a close eye on your ad performance and any notifications from Meta.

Quick Response: Address any issues or warnings promptly.

Continuous Optimization: Make necessary adjustments to improve your ad performance and compliance.

By following these guidelines, you can significantly reduce the risk of ad disapprovals and ensure that your campaigns deliver optimal results.

Navigating Algorithm Changes

- **Staying adaptable in a constantly evolving advertising environment.**

The advertising landscape is in a state of perpetual flux, driven by technological advancements, shifting consumer behaviours, and evolving regulatory frameworks. To thrive in this dynamic environment, businesses must cultivate a culture of adaptability.

Key Strategies for Adaptability:

1. **Embrace Continuous Learning:**
   - **Stay Updated:** Regularly monitor industry trends, emerging technologies, and consumer preferences.
   - **Attend Workshops and Conferences:** Network with peers and industry experts.
   - **Encourage Experimentation:** Foster a culture of innovation and risk-taking.

2. **Leverage Data-Driven Insights:**
   - **Utilize Analytics Tools:** Track campaign performance and identify areas for improvement.
   - **A/B Testing:** Experiment with different ad creatives, targeting strategies, and messaging.

- **Data-Informed Decision Making:** Use data to guide strategic choices.

3. **Build Strong Relationships:**
    - **Partner with Influencers:** Collaborate with individuals who can amplify your brand's message.
    - **Foster Client Relationships:** Prioritize open communication and responsiveness.
    - **Network with Industry Professionals:** Build a strong network of contacts.

4. **Adapt to New Platforms and Technologies:**
    - **Explore Emerging Channels:** Stay ahead of the curve by adopting new platforms like TikTok or Instagram Reels.
    - **Embrace AI and Automation:** Leverage AI-powered tools to streamline processes and enhance efficiency.
    - **Stay Updated on Privacy Regulations:** Ensure compliance with data privacy laws like GDPR and CCPA.

5. **Cultivate a Flexible Mindset:**
    - **Embrace Change:** View challenges as opportunities for growth.
    - **Adapt to Shifting Priorities:** Be prepared to pivot quickly when necessary.
    - **Foster a Culture of Agility:** Empower teams to make timely decisions.

By embracing these strategies, businesses can navigate the ever-changing advertising landscape, seize opportunities, and maintain a competitive edge.

10. Real-World Success Stories
Inspirational Case Studies

- **Examples of businesses that achieved remarkable growth through Meta campaigns.**

    Meta (formerly Facebook) has been a powerful platform for businesses of all sizes to achieve significant growth. Here are a few notable examples:

1. **Warby Parker:** This eyewear company leveraged Meta's precise targeting capabilities to reach a highly specific audience. By using detailed demographics and interests, they were able to drive a significant increase in online sales and brand awareness.

2. **Duolingo:** The language learning app utilized Meta's advertising solutions to acquire new users and re-engage existing ones. Through targeted campaigns and creative ad formats, they were able to boost app downloads and user retention.

3. **Allbirds:** The sustainable footwear brand successfully used Meta's dynamic product ads to showcase their products in a visually appealing way. By retargeting users who had previously visited their website, they were able to drive conversions and increase sales.

4. **Outdoor Voices:** This athletic apparel brand employed Meta's video ads to tell compelling brand stories and generate buzz. By creating engaging content that resonated with their target audience, they were able to build a loyal following and drive significant website traffic.

These are just a few examples of how businesses have leveraged Meta's advertising platform to achieve remarkable growth. By understanding your target audience, crafting compelling ad creative, and continuously optimizing your campaigns, you can unlock the full potential of Meta advertising for your business.

- **Key takeaways and replicable strategies from their journeys.**

Here are some key takeaways and replicable strategies inspired by the principles of Meta Marketing Mastery:

1. Know Your Audience Deeply:

Create Detailed Buyer Personas: Develop in-depth profiles of your target audience, including demographics, interests, and behaviours.

Leverage Meta's Advanced Targeting: Utilize tools like interest-based targeting, lookalike audiences, and custom audiences to reach the right people.

2. Craft Compelling Content:

Visual Storytelling: Use high-quality images and videos to capture attention and evoke emotions.

Engaging Copywriting: Write concise, persuasive copy that resonates with your audience.

Consistent Branding: Maintain a consistent brand voice and visual identity across all platforms.

3. Optimize for Mobile:

Mobile-First Approach: Design your ads and landing pages with mobile devices in mind.

Fast-Loading Pages: Ensure quick page load times to minimize bounce rates.

Easy-to-Use Mobile Experiences: Optimize for seamless user experiences on smartphones and tablets.

4. Harness the Power of Video:

Short-Form Video: Create engaging short-form videos for platforms like Instagram Reels and TikTok.

Live Video: Host live streams to connect with your audience in real-time.

Video Ads: Use video ads to tell your brand story and drive conversions.

5. Leverage User-Generated Content:

Encourage Sharing: Encourage customers to share their experiences with your brand on social media.

User-Generated Ad Campaigns: Incorporate user-generated content into your ad campaigns.

6. Measure and Iterate:

Track Key Metrics: Monitor key performance indicators like clicks, impressions, and conversions.

A/B Testing: Experiment with different ad variations to optimize performance.

Continuous Improvement: Regularly analyze your results and make data-driven adjustments.

By implementing these strategies and staying up-to-date with the latest trends in Meta advertising, you can achieve significant growth and success for your business.

11. The Future of Meta Campaigns

Emerging Trends

- **AR/VR ads, metaverse integrations, and the next frontier of Facebook marketing.**

    As technology continues to evolve, so does the landscape of digital advertising. Facebook, now known as Meta, is at the forefront of this evolution, pioneering the integration of Augmented Reality (AR), Virtual Reality (VR), and the metaverse into its marketing platform.

    Here's a breakdown of what this means for businesses:

    AR/VR Ads:

    - **Immersive Experiences:** AR/VR ads offer a unique opportunity to create immersive brand experiences. Users can virtually try on products, explore virtual showrooms, or interact with brand mascots in a 3D environment.

    - **Enhanced Engagement:** These ads can significantly boost engagement rates, as they provide a more interactive and memorable experience compared to traditional 2D ads.

    Metaverse Integrations:

    - **Virtual Brand Presence:** Brands can establish virtual storefronts, host virtual events, and interact with customers in a fully immersive digital world.

- **New Marketing Channels:** The metaverse opens up new marketing channels, such as virtual billboards, product placements in virtual worlds, and sponsored virtual experiences.

Why is this important for businesses?

Increased Brand Awareness: By leveraging AR/VR and the metaverse, businesses can reach a wider audience and create a stronger brand impression.

Enhanced Customer Engagement: Immersive experiences can foster deeper connections with customers, leading to increased brand loyalty and advocacy.

Innovative Marketing Campaigns: These technologies allow for creative and innovative marketing campaigns that stand out from the competition.

As the metaverse continues to develop, it's crucial for businesses to stay ahead of the curve and explore the potential of AR/VR and metaverse marketing. By embracing these emerging technologies, businesses can unlock new opportunities and drive significant growth.

- **Staying ahead of the curve with proactive strategies.**

In today's rapidly evolving business landscape, staying ahead of the curve is crucial for long-term success. Proactive strategies allow organizations to anticipate and respond to change, seize opportunities, and minimize risks. Here are some key strategies to consider:

1. Continuous Learning and Innovation:

Embrace a culture of learning: Encourage employees to acquire new skills and knowledge.

Foster innovation: Create a space for creativity and experimentation.

Stay updated on industry trends: Monitor industry news, attend conferences, and network with peers.

2. Data-Driven Decision Making:

Leverage data analytics: Use data to identify trends, optimize processes, and make informed decisions.

Invest in data infrastructure: Ensure you have the tools and technology to collect, analyze, and interpret data effectively.

3. Customer-Centric Approach:

Understand customer needs: Conduct market research and gather customer feedback.

Personalize customer experiences: Tailor products and services to individual preferences.

Build strong customer relationships: Foster loyalty through excellent customer service.

4. Risk Management:

Identify potential risks: Conduct regular risk assessments.

Develop contingency plans: Prepare for unexpected challenges.

Implement robust security measures: Protect your organization's assets and data.

5. Strategic Partnerships:

Collaborate with other businesses: Form strategic alliances to share resources and expertise.

Build strong relationships with suppliers: Ensure a reliable supply chain.

By implementing these proactive strategies, organizations can position themselves for future growth and success. Remember, the key to staying ahead of the curve is to be adaptable, innovative, and customer-focused.

12. Final Thoughts: Your Roadmap to Success

Summarize the core principles of creating and managing successful campaigns.

Creating and managing successful campaigns requires a strategic approach and a deep understanding of your target audience. Here are some core principles to keep in mind:

1. Clear and Measurable Objectives:

Define Goals: Clearly outline what you want to achieve with your campaign.

Set SMART Goals: Ensure your goals are Specific, Measurable, Achievable, Relevant, and Time-bound.

2. Know Your Target Audience:

Identify Demographics: Understand their age, gender, location, and interests.

Psychographics: Delve into their values, lifestyles, and behaviours.

Create Buyer Personas: Develop fictional representations of your ideal customers.

3. Develop a Strong Brand Message:

Unique Selling Proposition (USP): Highlight what sets you apart.

Consistent Branding: Maintain a consistent brand voice, tone, and visual identity.

4. Choose the Right Channels:

Select Platforms: Choose platforms that align with your target audience and campaign goals.

Multi-Channel Approach: Consider a combination of channels for maximum impact.

5. Create Compelling Content:

High-Quality Content: Produce engaging content that resonates with your audience.

Storytelling: Use storytelling techniques to connect with your audience emotionally.

Visual Appeal: Utilize visually appealing images and videos.

6. Effective Campaign Planning and Scheduling:

Timeline: Create a detailed timeline for each campaign phase.

Resource Allocation: Allocate resources efficiently to ensure timely execution.

Contingency Planning: Have a plan B for unexpected challenges.

7. Monitor and Analyze Performance:

Key Performance Indicators (KPIs): Track relevant metrics to measure success.

Data-Driven Insights: Use data to identify areas for improvement.

Continuous Optimization: Make adjustments based on performance data.

8. Build Strong Relationships:

Customer Engagement: Foster relationships with your audience through interaction.

Partnerships: Collaborate with other businesses to expand your reach.

Customer Feedback: Listen to customer feedback and incorporate it into your strategy.

By following these core principles, you can create and manage campaigns that deliver exceptional results and drive business growth.

Encourage your leads (prospective customers) to take immediate action and embrace experimentation.

1. Create a Sense of Urgency:

Limited-time offers: Highlight time-sensitive deals or discounts.

Scarcity principle: Emphasize limited availability of resources or opportunities.

Fear of missing out (FOMO): Create a sense of exclusivity and urgency.

2. Use Strong Calls to Action:

Direct and actionable language: Use verbs like "start," "try," or "discover."

Clear instructions: Guide readers step-by-step on what to do next.

Visually prominent CTAs: Use contrasting colors and clear button designs.

3. Highlight the Benefits:

Clear value proposition: Explain how readers will benefit from taking action.

Social proof: Share testimonials or case studies to build credibility.

Emotional appeal: Connect with readers' desires and aspirations.

4. Encourage Experimentation:

Low-risk starting points: Suggest small, manageable steps to begin with.

Celebrate failures: Frame failures as learning opportunities.

Share success stories: Inspire readers with examples of successful experiments.

5. Provide Support and Resources:

Offer guidance: Provide helpful tips, tutorials, or webinars.

Create a community: Foster a supportive environment for sharing experiences.

Provide tools and templates: Simplify the process of experimentation.

Closing motivational words to inspire long-term success.

Short and Sweet:

- "Remember, the journey of a thousand miles begins with a single step."
- "Your future self will thank you."
- "Believe in yourself, and you'll be unstoppable."
- "The only limit is the one you set."

Inspiring and Empowering:

- "The greatest glory is not in never falling, but in rising every time we fall."
- "Success is not final, failure is not fatal: It is the courage to continue that counts."
- "The only way to do great work is to love what you do."
- "The future belongs to those who believe in the beauty of their dreams."

Call to Action:

- "So, what are you waiting for? Start your journey today."
- "It's time to take control of your destiny."
- "Let's make this the year you achieve greatness."

    Remember, the key to effective motivation is authenticity and relevance. Tailor your closing words to the specific audience and context. By inspiring and empowering your listeners, you can motivate them to take action and achieve their goals.

FREE Bonus

You will get FREE access to the Author via e-mail to get any technical help while using or setting up Meta Facebook Ad Campaigns. Last but not the least you will become eligible to join the weekly live sessions of the Author which is part of a Premium Course launched by the Author.

Additional Sections

- **Recommended Resources**: Tools, platforms, and communities to enhance learning.

Comprehensive Guide to Signing Up and Setting Up a Meta Business Manager Account

Introduction

Meta Business Manager is a powerful tool that allows businesses to manage their Facebook and Instagram accounts, ad campaigns, and assets all in one place. Setting up an account properly ensures streamlined operations, secure management, and effective advertising. This guide provides a detailed, step-by-step walkthrough to sign up and set up your Meta Business Manager account for success.

Step 1: Prerequisites Before You Begin

Before setting up your Meta Business Manager account, ensure the following:

1. **A Personal Facebook Account**: You need an active Facebook account to create a Business Manager account.
2. **Business Details**: Gather the official name, email address, and website of your business.
3. **Access to Business Assets**: Ensure you have administrative access to your business's Facebook Page(s) and Ad Account(s).

Step 2: Signing Up for Meta Business Manager

1. **Visit the Meta Business Manager Website**: Go to business.facebook.com.
2. **Click on "Create Account"**:
   - On the homepage, locate the "Create Account" button and click it.

3. **Enter Business Details**:
   - Provide your business name.
   - Enter your work email address (preferably an official business email).
   - Add your business's official name and details like address and phone number.

4. **Submit the Form**:
   - Click "Next" after entering all necessary details.
   - Verify your email address using the confirmation link sent to your inbox.

Step 3: Setting Up Your Business Manager Account

A. Add Your Facebook Page(s)

1. **Navigate to Business Settings**:
   - On the left-hand menu, click "Business Settings."

2. **Add a Page**:
   - Click on "Accounts" > "Pages" > "Add".
   - Select one of the following options:
     - **Add a Page**: If you own the page.
     - **Request Access to a Page**: If you need admin or editor access.
     - **Create a New Page**: If your business doesn't already have a Facebook Page.

- **Sign in**: If you have already created your account earlier then you can follow the Sign in option.

3. **Confirm Ownership**:
    - Follow on-screen prompts to confirm your role in managing the Page.

B. Add or Create Ad Accounts

1. **Locate Ad Accounts**:
    - Go to "Accounts" > "Ad Accounts" > "Add".

2. **Choose One of Three Options**:
    - **Add an Ad Account**: If you already have one created.
    - **Request Access**: If someone else owns the account.
    - **Create a New Ad Account**: For businesses new to advertising.

3. **Set Permissions**:
    - Assign roles like "Admin," "Advertiser," or "Analyst" for team members who will manage the Ad Account.

C. Assign Team Members and Roles

1. **Add People**:
    - Go to "Users" > "People" > "Add".
    - Enter the email addresses of your team members.

2. **Assign Roles**:
   - Choose roles such as "Employee Access" or "Admin Access."
   - Assign specific asset permissions (e.g., Page management, Ad account management).

D. Add Payment Methods

1. **Navigate to Payment Settings**:
   - In Business Settings, click "Payments" > "Add Payment Method."

2. **Provide Payment Details**:
   - Enter your preferred payment method (credit/debit card, PayPal, etc.).
   - Ensure the billing address matches your business address.

3. **Set Spending Limits**:
   - You can set account spending limits to control your advertising expenses.

Step 4: Integrating Instagram Accounts

1. **Go to Instagram Accounts Section**:
   - In Business Settings, click "Accounts" > "Instagram Accounts."

2. **Add Your Instagram Account**:
   - Click "Add" and log in to your Instagram account.

- Ensure your Instagram account is converted to a Business Profile.

3. **Connect to Facebook Pages**:
   - Link your Instagram account to the relevant Facebook Page for seamless management.

Step 5: Verifying Your Business

1. **Locate Business Info**:
   - In Business Settings, click "Business Info" at the bottom left of the menu.

2. **Submit Verification Details**:
   - Provide official documents like a utility bill, tax identification number, or business registration certificate.

3. **Await Approval**:
   - Verification may take several days. You'll receive updates via email.

Step 6: Organizing Assets for Efficient Management

1. **Use Asset Groups**:
   - Create groups of Pages, Ad Accounts, and Pixels for different projects or campaigns.

2. **Set Permissions by Asset**:
   - Tailor access levels for team members to ensure security and accountability.

Step 7: Setting Up Pixels and Events

1. **Go to Data Sources**:

- In Business Settings, click "Data Sources" > "Pixels."
2. **Create a Pixel**:
   - Follow prompts to generate a Pixel ID.
3. **Install Pixel Code**:
   - Add the Pixel code to your website using manual installation or via an integration partner like Shopify or WordPress.
4. **Set Up Events**:
   - Use the Event Setup Tool to define key actions (e.g., purchases, signups) on your website.

Step 8: Securing Your Business Manager Account

1. **Enable Two-Factor Authentication**:

   - Go to "Security Center" > "Two-Factor Authentication" and require it for all users.

2. **Regularly Review User Activity**:

   - Monitor asset usage and revoke access for inactive team members.

Conclusion

Setting up a Meta Business Manager account is the first step toward unlocking the full potential of Meta's advertising ecosystem. By following these steps, you can ensure a secure, organized, and effective management system for your business's Facebook and Instagram marketing efforts. Once everything is set up, you're ready to launch campaigns that drive results and propel your business toward growth!

www.ingramcontent.com/pod-product-compliance
Lightning Source LLC
Chambersburg PA
CBHW071051240526
45469CB00006BD/2297